GLEN KELLY REAL ESATE, LLC AND GLEN KELLY REALTORS PRESENTS

Understanding

New Jersey Real Estate

By

Glen Kelly

Broker of Record

Table of Contents

Chapter 1 - Introduction

Glen Kelly's Personal Introduction

Chapter 2 – Real Estate Accolades

Understanding Realtor credentials and accolades

Chapter 3 – Listing and Selling

Listing Your Home for Sale in New Jersey

Benefits of using a Realtor to Sell

How to select a Realtor

Chapter 4 – Purchasing a Home

What to do when you start viewing homes

What to look for when viewing a home

Getting pre-approved for a mortgage

Offers, Contracts & Attorney Reviews

Chapter 5 – Home Inspections

Choosing a Home Inspector

Types of Home Inspections

Repair Requests

Chapter 6 – NJ Appraisals, Property Surveys and Flood Elevation Certifications

NJ Appraisals

How to get a high appraisal

During the Appraisal: What to do and what you need

What to do if you get a low appraisal

Property Surveys

Flood Elevation Certifications

Chapter 7 – Mortgage Commitments

    Mortgage Commitments

    Reasons to hire a Licensed Mortgage Broker

    What makes a good Mortgage Broker

Chapter 8 – Home owner and Flood Insurance

    What you need for Home Owners Insurance

    Flood Insurance

Chapter 9 – Certificate of Occupancy Inspection

    Certificate of Occupancy (CO)

    Certificate of Continued Occupancy (CCO)

Chapter 10 – Mortgage Payoffs, Walkthrough Inspection and Closings

    Mortgage Pay off Statement

    Walk- through Inspection

    Closings

    HUD Statement

Chapter 11 – New Construction

    New Construction

    Finding a good Builder

    Signs of a good Builder

    Finding a lot to build on

    Phases of new construction

Chapter 12 – Shorts Sales and Foreclosures

    Short Sales

    Foreclosures

Chapter 13 – Careers in Real Estate

    Starting a career in Real Estate

Chapter 14 - Conclusion

    Conclusion

Chapter 1

Introduction

Welcome to my wonderful world of real estate. I'm Glen Kelly, Broker of Record of Glen Kelly Real Estate LLC, also known as Glen Kelly, Realtors. I have been intricately involved in the Monmouth and Ocean County New Jersey real estate market for over 15 years. I bought my first property at the age of 20, rehabbed it back to splendor, sold it not long after and I have not looked back since.

In addition to obtaining my New Jersey Broker's License and multiple collegiate degrees, I've also earned my SFR®, SRES®, and CRS®, the latter of which is obtained by only 3 percent of

REALTORS®. I have a long-standing background in construction, and apprenticed under my father, John Kelly, who is a master carpenter and a New Jersey Licensed New Home Builder. The combination of hands-on experience in carpentry and real estate, as well as formal education, has helped to make me a leader in my field.

Over the years, I've put all my time, drive and passion into real estate; then created and hand tailored Glen Kelly Real Estate LLC to make it a successful business that values customer satisfaction above all else. In order to create a streamlined and more personal approach to my business, I opted for one centralized executive main office in Beachwood, New Jersey rather than several different branches all over the state.

Despite the Ocean County physical location, Glen Kelly Real Estate LLC services New Jersey as a whole with a concentration in Ocean and Monmouth County. While specializing in new construction, waterfront, and luxury homes, we more importantly dedicate ourselves in helping you sell your home or find the perfect new one.

Glen Kelly Real Estate, as well as the man behind it, delivers a commitment to excellence that's unparalleled. Whether you are selling or buying a home or simply have questions about how to get started, you'll receive top notch customer service that you will not find anywhere else.

Chapter 2

Real Estate Accolades

Short Sales and Foreclosure Resource (SFR®) Specialist

A SFR® specialist is someone who receives a Short Sales and Foreclosure Resource certification from the National Association of REALTORS® to be a trusted resource to help you deal with short sales and foreclosures. As the Broker of Record of Glen Kelly Real Estate, this special designation is something I hold in high regard. Being a SFR® certified REALTOR® means a lot in this business. I make sure I teach the spectrum of this degree to my agents. All of my agents are well versed in Short Sales and Foreclosures and must attend mandatory training and continuing education on said topic as required by Glen Kelly Real Estate.

So how does this benefit you? When you are facing a short sale or foreclosure, you want an agent who knows what they are doing, will answer all your questions, and essentially be your advocate to help you through the situation in the best way possible. A SFR® specialist will help you find financial and legal counselors, negotiate with lenders on your behalf, limit your amount of risk, qualify sellers for short sales and protect you and your rights overall. When you have a SFR® specialist by your side, you can expect a much smoother process.

Seniors Real Estate Specialist (SRES®)

According to the National Association of Realtors (NAR), the average age of repeat buyers is about 51, which means now more than ever, those 50 and over are looking for new or additional homes. This is where a SRES® agent comes in. They are specially trained in the Seniors Real Estate Specialist (SRES®) Designation Course by REALTORS® to assist in the needs of the buyers and sellers who are 50+.

The course focuses on counseling and supporting that demographic through the home buying and selling process rather than fixating on how to sell a home to them. SRES® agents are well versed on tax laws, estate planning, relocating and refinancing for the 50+ crowd. With a difficult decision such as selling the family home, the SRES® agent can help you through the bittersweet process.

Every agent at Glen Kelly Real Estate is taught the fundamentals of this designation by me. I am proud to be a licensed SRES® agent and my team of real estate professionals can help you with any of your senior real estate needs whether you are buying or selling a home.

Certified Residential Specialist (CRS®)

CRS® specialists are the best-of-the-best in terms of business education, negotiations, time management, efficiency, customer support and business planning. It is the highest credential level awarded to real estate brokers, managers and sales agents. Only about 3 percent of REALTORS® hold this distinguished title and they are three times more successful in sales than their counterparts. They have an incredible amount of up-to-date knowledge on the current real estate market that is not found just anywhere. You know when you are dealing with a CRS® agent that you are going to get quality and top notch results.

Buying or selling a home is one of the biggest decisions you will ever make in your life regardless of how many times you go through the process. Do you really want to trust the experience to just any agent or would you rather deal with a CRS® specialist, someone who is one of the best in their field? I am a CRS® specialist who can help you through the home buying and selling process with expert knowledge that will get you the best results.

Every agent at Glen Kelly Real Estate is required to fulfill continuing education and mandatory company training sessions that teaches the core principals of this very prestigious title.

Chapter 3

Listing and Selling

Listing your home or property in New Jersey

A good broker will provide money and time to get your property out there and noticed by prospective buyers. From listing it online to talking about it with fellow Realtors, the more methods of marketing your agent utilizes and the more people who hear about your home, the more likely it will sell. However, it is up to you to contribute and make an effort on your end as well. The best way to get results is to take it step-by-step, think about things clearly, make the right adjustments, and work as a team with your real estate agent in order to complete a successful sale of your home.

Listing Home or Property Tips

When it comes to listing a home or property, it is not as easy as taking a few pictures, throwing together a half-hearted description, and putting it up on a website. It's important to carefully think things through, make the right moves at the right time, and look at your home through the eyes of a buyer. There are several tips to keep in mind when you are listing your home or properties that can help you keep your sanity and allow you to sell your home in a timely manner.

Sell at the right time - The slowest time frame to sell your home is during the holidays. Customers may not consider making a major purchase, with the budget constraints present at this time. Besides, who wants to spend the weeks surrounding the holidays packing up boxes and getting ready to move when they could be spending that precious time with family. A better time to start marketing your property is right after the holidays, before spring time when the beauty of landscaping is at its peak. There are quite a few people who think ahead to the summer months when they can take vacation days off of work and devote time to the moving process.

If you do need to sell and spring is not an option, you can still get a good market value for your property, but you absolutely must strategize with your agent. A good agent, coupled with a great broker, can sell homes regardless of the time period. Buyers that are looking for homes and properties outside of the traditional time of showings are buyers that are very serious. There is also an entire class of buyers called investors that will gladly make offers on any home or property regardless of the time period in question. Key point to remember here is to list your home or property with a qualified, professional Realtor.

Choose the right agent - Ask family and friends for real estate agent referrals, and then do a little digging online to check out their reviews. Zillow is a good place to start, and it is also where you can view my company's page and read through our five-star reviews. I cannot stress enough how important it is to choose the right agent / broker. Ask your agent or broker to supply references. If you choose an agent that is going to put in minimal effort and does not act in a professional manner, you are not going to get the results you need and want and could end up having more headaches than you bargained for. Before you sign, ask about the agents' background, degrees, designations, production, and see their reviews online. When you sign a listing agreement you are placing the ultimate trust in that one broker and specifically that agent which should not be taken lightly. Your agent and the agents' broker will be the magical force behind selling your home or property. Many brokers ask you for a six month to one year listing of your home or property. Ask yourself, am I ok with locking the marketing of my home with this agent for six months? One year? As a seller you deserve the best in the business. Checking details upfront will save you a lot of time, money, and frustration. Remember, every agent / broker is not the same; you will be glad you did your homework. Lastly, always remember that a very large majority of real estate agents are part-time, working real estate outside of their regular job. Do yourself a favor and hire someone that does real estate as a full time career. Someone that eats, sleeps, and breathes real estate. You will thank me if you do.

Clean, clean, clean - Everything has to be cleaned from top-to-bottom, including under the sinks, behind the drapes, and in drawers. There should not be any cobwebs, rolling dust bunnies or thin layers of dirt on your ceiling fans. Hire a cleaning service if you have to; just make sure the cleaning is completely thorough. Many cleaning services will give a discount to first time clients, so make sure to let them know if you are one when you call. Bottom line is the home should be clean. No buyer wants to see a dirty home.

Clear out the clutter - You already know that your home should be clean, but did you know you should de-clutter everything, including your junk drawers and the tops of your closets? Yes, even the hidden spots have to be de-cluttered. Of course everything has to look neat and tidy for the pictures, but you should also expect that buyers might look in every nook and cranny of your home. Get rid of all the little things in your house that do not visually enhance the space; even if that means you have to pack everything in boxes and temporarily put it in storage. You do not have to go crazy here, but if you have a lot of little items all over the place and it looks cluttered, then pack it! Remember the idea here is to have your home look as clean and spacious as possible. Having a dirty or cluttered home can actually deter a buyer from making an offer.

Organize everything - Cleaning and clearing out the clutter are just the first two steps in making your home look presentable. Next up is organizing everything, from the shelves in your bathroom to the towels in your linen closet. Treat your home as if it were a model property, where everything has a place and is right where it should be. Organization of your home will make your home appear to be more appetizing to any buyer. Coupled with cleanliness and no clutter, you will be on your way to a successful showing.

Round up faux potential buyers - You can drive past your property and do a walkthrough of your home, but most likely you are going to be a bit biased. This is where trusted family and friends can come in. Ask them to act as potential buyers, drive past your home, inspect the property, and do a tour of the home as if they were real potential home buyers. Have them tell you where you can make some improvements. This way when the real buyers come, your home looks top notch. Your agent can give you a detailed analysis of how your home or property compares to similar near-by comparable properties.

Make the improvements - Are there improvements you need to make or that your real estate agent wants you to do? If so, get them done before the house goes on the market. You do not want to wait until buyers already start trickling in. Talk to your real estate agent about recommendations for professionals, such as a new painter or plumber. This will save you time, energy, and money from having to do the search yourself. Do not go overboard. I have heard some crazy things from sellers over the years of what agents recommended prior to listing their home. Rip down trim and replace with crown molding; remove a deck and replace with a new treks deck; rip up the asphalt and replace with a new concrete driveway; the list is endless. The key is no buyer is walking away from your home over ridiculous nonsense items like changing the trim. So if your agent stresses a lot of updates prior to marketing your home, this should be a red flag and you may want to get a second opinion.

Depersonalize - The family photos, magazines, and displayed photo albums may have to go. They make the house a home, which is a problem when you are trying to make your home someone else's house. It's best to remove most of the personal mementos, box them up, and store them where they will not be seen. Even if you cannot stand to pack all of them up, at least get some down and packed away.

Be realistic about price - The market fluctuates all the time, so you have to be realistic in terms of price. There are some buyers who believe their house is worth far more than what the real estate agent believes is the proper listing price. A good real estate agent wants the best price for your home. If they give you a dollar amount you are not pleased with, ask for their reasoning behind it before you immediately shoot it down. Remember the price of your home is going to compare against recent sales of like and or similar homes in the area. No matter what price is determined, if your home does not sell in 3-4 months then it is most likely overpriced and needs a price drop.

Listen to your agent - Agents will be giving you suggestions about your home that is based on a non-biased perspective. The decision is ultimately yours, but this is why you want to choose an agent that is reputable so you know that what they are saying is really in your best interest.

Benefits of Using a Realtor to Sell

There are many who feel that selling their home for sale by owner (FSBO) is the way to go, but it could be a big mistake. It can take money out of your pocket, give you more frustrations than you could imagine, and leave your house sitting on the market for years. Consider all the benefits of using a real estate agent rather than going it alone and you may find it's the best option for you in the short and long run. Selling your home or property is not as easy as one thinks. It takes a professional to show you the best ways. There is a lot of time and money that goes into selling any property.

No piles of paperwork - Until you've seen the piles of paperwork a real estate agent has to deal with, you will likely say it is probably not too big a deal, when in actuality, it can all make your head spin. Why would you want to add all that paperwork to your to-do list when you can let a trained real estate agent take care of all of it for you so you do not have to?

Access to more resources - Real estate agents have access to websites you've probably never even heard of or have the ability to use. Not only do they have the ability to access these sites, but it also means you do not have to do all the leg work yourself.

Access to numerous connections - When you hire a real estate agent, you are not just hiring one person; it's more like you are hiring a network of professionals. They talk to each other, discuss properties, and work together for the good of their clients – at least the reputable agents do. Find a real estate agent that knows how to work as part of a team, like those at Glen Kelly Real Estate, and you'll have much better results than if you try to go it alone.

Agents know what works - When walking through your home and property, real estate agents will point out what you need to change or fix, and what you can do to draw in even more buyers. When you go to sell on your own, you may have a biased opinion, which will not be as beneficial against a professional agent's opinion, especially one that has been in the real estate industry for years and knows what works.

Legal and financial protection - When doing a FSBO, you are putting yourself at risk for legal and financial problems you may never have even seen coming. Using a real estate agent you are protected. They can help you deal with any issues should a problem arise or even prevent them in the first place.

Agents are expert negotiators - Agents know what they are doing more than you may think. Buyers are tough negotiators nowadays, especially with all the information that's readily available at their fingertips. The last thing you want is to accept a low-ball offer instead of what you really deserve for your home. Go with a real estate agent who knows the real estate market inside and out, as well as what your home is really worth. This insures the correct amount of sale value.

They know how to market - There are a plethora of options that real estate agents use to market your home that are more difficult, time consuming and costly for you to do on your own. They know what will and will not work for your particular home and neighborhood, and what's going to get you the best results.

Less time commitment on your part - Between the marketing, communications with buyers, doing tours of your home; selling your home is a huge time commitment. Getting it ready for sale is time consuming enough; do you really want to add more to the list? When you hire a real estate agent, they are specifically trained to handle the day-to-day maneuverings of a real estate transaction in a timely manner. Take it all on yourself along with everything else you have to do and you may be begging for a real estate agent to take the hassle off your hands.

It's safer for you - Do you really want to have a bunch of strange people coming into your home so you can show them around the place? When you go through a realtor, it is customary to pre-screen the prospective buyers so they know who they are dealing with. You do not want to put yourself at risk simply for the sake of selling your home.

They can help you find repair professionals - Real estate agents are excellent sources for finding those who can do repairs and adjustments on your home if you need them. When you get recommendations from the real estate professional you are dealing with, you know they come from a trusted source. Ask for several and then do your own research to find reviews as well as have consultations. This will save you a ton of time and energy.

How to Select a Realtor

If only selecting a realtor was as easy as pointing to a name and knowing you'll end up with someone reputable. Selling your home is no easy task, nor is it something to be taken lightly, so choosing the right realtor is incredibly important. You want someone who has your back, knows what they are doing, and is going to get you excellent results. So how exactly do you go about picking the perfect realtor?

Ask for personal recommendations - The first step you should take when looking for a realtor is to ask your family and friends. Next, thanks to social media, a simple post or tweet can net you a slew of recommendations from those who have already been through the process.

Check that they are licensed - Every state has their own professional licensing bureau for real estate agents, so before you commit to someone, check first that they are properly licensed. For example, if you are from New Jersey, a simple Google search of "New Jersey professional real estate licensing bureau" will pull up the New Jersey Real Estate Commission website. On the left side of the front page is an option called "licensee search" which will bring you to another window. Click on "Real Estate" search, enter in the agent's name, such as Glen Kelly, and you'll be able to see whether or not they are actively licensed.

Choose by credentials - Real estate agents may have certain abbreviations on their business card, but they are just a bunch of random letters until you know what they mean. Depending on your particular situation, they can be incredibly important. For example, if you are someone 50+, you should consider using a real estate agent who is a Senior Real Estate Specialist (SRES). Should the agent use a capital "R" in realtor (REALTOR®) rather than a lower case that means they are a member of the National Association of Realtors® and adhere to their code of ethics.

Contact several realtors – Do not be afraid to reach out to several realtors to see what they can do for you because you do not have to commit right away. Compare them all side-by-side. Do some research to find out which one you feel is best, and then trust your instincts. If a real estate agent complains or gives you an ultimatum if they find out you are choosing amongst a handful, walk away! If an agent blatantly bad mouths another agent or firm, walk away! A real professional agent that's worth it is not going to pressure you, but will instead be confident in their ability and trust that you will be making the right decision by finding the best real estate agent for you. Remember, your home or property is more than likely your biggest asset. Treat it as such and only offer it to a professional.

Read the reviews - Most real estate agents, like Glen Kelly, have pages on Zillow where you can read reviews and ratings on everything from their level of knowledge to their negotiation skills. You can also read an "About Me" section and get access to all their contact information.

Ask for referrals and testimonials - You can read some referrals and testimonials online, but do not hesitate to ask for additional ones. Any professional and reputable real estate agent will not hesitate to hand them over or at least provide you with the number of a client who can give you a personal reference.

Ask the hard questions – Do not be afraid to write down a series of questions and ask each one to any selected Realtor. Those who are worth it will have no problem putting the time aside to answer them. If they can't, then they likely will not do so during the house hunting process either. You are better off finding this out sooner than later. One good question to ask is "How many homes have you listed and or sold in the past year?" You can find out a lot just from that question alone, including how much time they devote to each perspective buyer / seller as well as how successful they are at their job.

Trust your instinct - You can do all the work you want, do as much research as you can handle, but in the end, it's all about trusting your instinct. If something just does not feel right, move onto someone else. Often, that instinct and feeling can tell you much more than searching for information ever could.

What Glen Kelly Real Estate (GKRE) can do for you?

Glen Kelly has more than 15 years' experience in the real estate industry, and that's just the start. As part of GKRE, he has a team behind him that can help you sell your home with ease and in a timely manner. When you choose an agent from GKRE, you gain a team of allies who are going to have your back and walk you through the home selling process. They do not settle for knowing just the basics about the real estate industry; they have a thirst for knowledge and a strong drive for excellence. Glen Kelly has the distinct honor of being a SFR® specialist, a SRES® specialist, and also being a CRS® agent. GKRE is all about quality, results, and satisfaction. At the end of the day, you'll have a real estate experience that will make you proud of your decision to sign on with GKRE.

The first steps you take when selling your home or property can be overwhelming. Not only are you dealing with the bittersweet decision to sell your home, but you also have to prep your current home for sale, navigate a move, and deal with all the financial aspects. GKRE can help you take much of the burden off your shoulders by streamlining the process and making it as easy for you as possible.

Chapter 4

Purchasing a home

You've found your realtor, you know what type of home you want, and have established your budget. Now you are ready to tour homes you select. The process may seem simple enough, but rarely will you immediately find the perfect house. Considering the huge monetary investment, you want to make sure you do the home-buying process correctly and efficiently, from how you tour the home to what you look for when you get there. There is also the mortgage phase and paperwork to process. Do not let it overwhelm you; take things step-by-step and before long, you'll have the home of your dreams.

What to do when starting to view homes

Your real estate agent is going to help you find homes that would be a good fit for you, but you can also do a search on your own and report back. The home-buying process can be intimidating, and the excitement of buying a new place can spur you to rush the process, but do not get ahead of yourself. When you are starting to view homes, there are several things to keep in mind that can help you find a place you love that's worth the money and time investment that you put into it.

Find a realtor you trust - The relationship between you and a realtor is like the one between yourself and your significant other; if you do not trust each other, you should not be together. Trust is essential, especially considering there's a lot of time and a substantial amount of money involved. You have to truly know that your real estate agent has your best interests in mind, and that they are not going to do anything that could be detrimental to you personally or financially.

Get pre-approved for a mortgage - Getting that pre-approval can make the process easier and it can help you learn how much you can really afford to spend on a house. The decision is based on your financial standing including your income, credit history, and amount of debt. You'll need a handful of financial information, such as W2s, tax returns, pay stubs, bank statements, and anything else your lender asks for. Lenders issue the pre-approval letters, which are typically valid for up to 90 days, after 24-48 hours of receiving the application.

Take your time - It's understandable why you would want the home-buying process over as soon as possible. Of course it's exciting, but after the first handful of homes, you just want to find one you love and move on in. However, it's important that you take your time to really find a house that you can wake up happy in every morning and really turn it into your home you could not do without.

Do not take too long to make a decision - While you should not rush the home-buying process, you also don't want to take forever if you find a home you love. If you do not make a decision quick enough, someone could grab the place right out from under you. To help combat indecisiveness, make a list of everything you need a home to have then once you do a tour, check off things from the list as you go along. While this can help you, it is even more important to trust your decision. Ask yourself if you can picture waking up in the home every day and going to sleep in it every night.

Do not settle for just any house - The house-hunting process could take a while, likely months. Do not just give in and settle for a place that seems to relatively meet your needs. Some do so out of desperation or frustration, but acting on those temporary feelings could result in long term problems. You do not want to end up stuck with a house you are not thrilled with simply because you settled.

Do not be afraid to ask questions - If you do not understand something, do not hesitate to ask your real estate agent. That's what they are there for! Any good realtor will be happy to answer any question you have regardless of how ridiculous you may think it is. If you do not feel comfortable enough with your real estate agent to ask questions, maybe it's time to find a new one.

Research the house - Your real estate agent is going to research the property, but it never hurts to do a little digging on your own. The history of the house is important, especially if it's decades or hundreds of years old. It's understandable that you'd want to make sure nothing happened in the house that you are not yet aware of. In many cases, a simple look around the Internet could turn up results if there's anything to be found.

Do not schedule rush tours - One of the worst things you can do is schedule a tour of a home when you or your agent has to run off somewhere else not long after arriving. You may walk into a house and instantly love it, but further inspection could turn up things you are not thrilled with in the least, and if you do not give yourself the time to look, you may commit before you ever find them.

Do not eat or drink while doing tours - It's tempting to walk around with a coffee or granola bar in hand while you do tours, especially if it's early in the morning, but you do not want to accidentally spill or drop something and you also do not want to have to keep running to the bathroom.

Look up crime rates - The house you find may be beautiful, but it's typically not worth it if you have to live in a high crime area. You do not want to be afraid to walk the streets or play in your front yard, especially if you have a family. To find out what the crime rates are like in the area you'd like to live in, check out city-data.com, or other similar sites, which will give you a rundown of the different crimes, from arson to robbery, that have happened over the past decade or so. In addition, do an Internet search to get specific recent news articles about crimes that have occurred.

Do not look at homes that are over budget – You are going to come across homes that are gorgeous and seem perfect for you but are way too expensive. Your instincts are to want to do a tour of the house anyway, but refrain from doing so. It's only going to do one of two things: you are either going to get depressed about not being able to currently afford it or you are going to give in, go over budget and buy a home you can't afford.

Think long term – Do not buy a home with the thought process that you'll live in it only until you can buy another one. Buy it because you believe it's a place you can live in for a long time. Even if you do not have kids yet, you should look into an area that has an excellent school system. Should you choose a place based on your current living situation, and you fall in love with the home and area, you are going to find yourself in a huge predicament down the road if things change.

Research and tour the neighborhood - The neighborhood you live in is even more important than the house itself. Is there a highway nearby that will cause you many sleepless nights due to the noise? Is it a crime-ridden area? These are just two of the things you need to consider when you are researching the neighborhood. You want to live in an area that you really feel comfortable in and that compliments your lifestyle and who you are, not one that hinders it or makes you feel unsafe.

Get an inspection report - If you find a house that seems of interest to you, do not hesitate to ask for an inspection report if one exists. You are going to get one on your own anyway, but getting an extra one from the current owners if available does not hurt. Before you sign on the dotted line or invest in a house that will not be good to make your home, you want to make sure it's safe and you are getting your money's worth.

Do a self-inspection - In addition to getting a professional inspection, it's important to do one on your own. Not just on the layout of the home or the cleanliness of the property, but in all the little areas such as under the sinks and in the crawl spaces of the attic. You can make a check list to carry with you as you go along to make sure you cover everything you want.

What to look for when viewing a home

You can't just rely on your realtor to check everything out when you are walking through the home. After all, you are the one who's going to be living there. There are those who think simply going by gut and taking a few glances around will suffice, but you'd be surprised how crafty some homeowners can be when they are desperate to sell their home and have some rather unsightly defects to hide. If you get a good feeling from the home and feel it might be right for you, it's up to you to take things a step further by inspecting everything from the floors to the ceiling. To make things easier, write a list of where you should look in the house, and as you go along, make notes on each aspect of the home.

Look under area rugs - Rugs can hide a lot, especially area rugs. It's easy to throw one over a spot that got damaged and forget about it, so while you are walking around, do not be afraid to pick up area rugs and look underneath them for damage you were not told about.

Move furniture - Just like area rugs, furniture can hide a lot of damage not only on the floor, but on the walls as well. While you are not likely to move furniture while you are touring a home, definitely move the furniture around a bit when you have your inspections on the property to see if there's any secret damage you can't immediately see.

Check the heating and cooling - If you tour the house in the winter, you'll get an idea of how the heat works as it will likely be on, but what about the fans and air conditioning? Ask if they can be turned on while you are there so you can make sure they work. You do not want it to be months later after you've already signed on the dotted line to find out you have to make repairs.

View the roof - Step outside; walk to the sidewalk as well as across the street and take a look at the roof from all angles. If there are missing or warped shingles, it's a sign that there might be or has been some roof damage. The cost of replacing a roof varies, but can cost in the thousands of dollars. If you check the roof first and notice damage, it could save you quite a chunk of change.

Try out all the windows and doors - They may not seem very important in the grand scheme of things, but they are actually more so than you might think. Not only can loose windows and doors slam shut on fingers, but they can also cause your utility bills to skyrocket. Depending on the season, all that hot or cool air will escape through and you'll end up with a huge bill in return. Even more importantly are safety concerns. If the doors or windows do not lock properly, it can be very easy for someone to break in. Also, doors and windows that do not open or close properly could mean structural issues. While it's not always easy to spot if window frames are rotted, there's a little easy test that can help you determine whether or not they are. Press something hard into it, such as a screwdriver. If it easily presses in and makes a mark, it's a sign that they need to be replaced. Again, this should be inspected by a NJ licensed home inspector.

Look for water damage - Water can be incredibly detrimental to the home, especially if it's leaking into the house over a period of time. If the windows have condensation on them when it's raining and they are closed, it means water vapor is seeping in and they need to be replaced. Look for bubbling or cracking in the paint, especially on the ceiling. It typically means there's been water damage. If there are large cracks on the outside of the home, it means water has an easy access point in. Lastly, take a deep breath as you walk through each room. Should you catch a musty scent, it could mean mold is growing due to water damage.

Check the banisters - You do not want to worry about leaning on a banister one day and having it give way from underneath you, or even worse, out from under one of your children. If the banister shakes back and forth, it's a sign it needs to be immediately fixed before a serious incident takes place.

Try out appliances - Should appliances be up for sale along with the house, such as the refrigerator, dishwasher, clothes washer and dryer, ask if you can do a test run. You do not want to shell out the money for them and be under the impression that they are going to work correctly only to find out that dish soap streams out through the bottom of the dishwasher when it runs or the dryer rattles like boulders are in it even during the lightest loads. If the homeowners want you to purchase the appliances, they should have zero problems letting you try them out first.

Inspect the porch or deck - Just like with banisters, the porch and deck should be checked for the safety of your family. Look at the support posts, stairs, and beams for signs of rot, shake the railing back and forth, and make sure the deck or porch is securely attached to the house. While you are at it, find out how many people it can hold so you are aware ahead of time in case you decide to host a gathering.

Test out the stairs - All of stairs, inside and out, need to be checked for safety. Look for rot or sagging, and make sure you can't see any light shining through in the back where the stairs connect to each other. It can be a sign that they are coming apart from the backing and are no longer safe to walk on.

Inspect the foundation - The first way to know if something is off with the foundation is by checking if the floor is level on the inside. One investor years ago said to put a marble on one end of the floor, without pushing it, let it go. If it rolls across, it means the floor is not completely level. Make your way outside to inspect the foundation and check for cracks and deterioration. Should the foundation have small cracks, you may be able to easily repair them; however, it's the larger cracks that could be a big problem. Horizontal cracks are the most detrimental. Before you sign the papers to purchase the home, a specialized inspector should stop by to check everything.

Walk around the property - The area around the house should be as neat, safe, and tidy as the inside of the home, and if it's not ask for it to be cleaned up or fixed. Keep an eye out for poisonous plants, such as poison ivy or sumac. Should there be stone walkways on the property, make sure none of the stones are loose as it can create a danger if your foot gets caught and you trip. There should also be no debris, such as abandoned cars, wood planks, broken down greenhouses sheds and swing sets. While you are at it, take a look at the soil. If you are big on gardening, you'll want to make sure the dirt is in excellent shape for growing plants and vegetables.

Getting pre-approved for a mortgage

Getting pre-approved for a mortgage means you have a letter from a lender that's good for 60-90 days that gives you an idea how much you can afford to spend for a home. It also means you can look at houses in your price range, and only your price range, so you are not encouraged to spend more than you should or waste your time touring houses you can't afford. When you make an offer on a home, the pre-approval letter also makes it seem more legit and serious than if you were to make the offer without it. So how exactly do you go about getting pre-approved for a mortgage? The best answer to this question is to ask your Realtor, but here are some steps to take.

Shop lenders - Never settle for the first lender you choose; you should always talk to at least two or three before you make your final choice. Give each of them the same list of what you need, and then ask what they can do for you in terms of rates. While you are talking to each one, pay attention to how personable they are and how much you trust them. If you do not get a good feeling, move on to someone else. The mortgage broker business is a customer service orientated field and you deserve the absolute best in customer service.

Gather all the necessary documents – You are going to need to hand over about as much paperwork for pre-approval as you would if you were straight out applying for a mortgage. Among the list of papers you will need are bank statements, W2s, pay stubs, tax returns, asset documentation, and, if you are self-employed, profit and loss statements. Make copies of all the paperwork for your reference, mark down when you mailed it in or dropped it off, and keep it in a file where you have easy access to it should you immediately need to get your hands on it.

Check your credit report and score - Both play a huge part in getting pre-approved for a mortgage. Make a request for your credit report and check for any discrepancies. Should you notice any, take care of them immediately. In addition, let your lender know that you are taking care of them. Once you find out your credit score, you can start getting it up to a higher number if necessary and decide whether you want to proceed with pre-approval or wait a bit until you get your number up more.

Ask questions - If there's anything you do not understand about the pre-approval or the mortgage process, do not be afraid to ask. That's what your real estate agent and lender are there for. Do not wait until after you've signed on the line. Do it beforehand, especially so you can give yourself enough time to do your own research as well if you feel it's necessary.

If you find you can't get pre-approved, your best bet is to increase your credit score and decrease your amount of debt, then reapply. Your lender should also be able to give you personalized advice based your particular situation.

Rely on your Realtor to recommend a quality, professional mortgage broker. Agents interact with mortgage brokers on a daily basis so they can help you weed out the lesser of the bunch.

Offers, Contracts, and Attorney Review

After months of searching, researching, and tours, you are finally ready to make an offer on the home of your dreams. Three things that stand in your way from getting the house you want are making an offer, getting the contracts processed, and the attorney review. Do everything efficiently, correctly, and in a smart manner and you could end up walking away with the keys to the home of your dreams.

Making an Offer - Pre-approval certainly helps when making an offer on a home. If you can pay in all cash, you are in an even better position. Before you even make an offer, you must have your down payment on hand and ready to go. When it comes to deciding on the amount, consider how much other similar homes in the area have sold for, the reason the seller is moving, and the neighborhood environment. Find out whether or not there are any other offers on the table. Think about the condition of the house, and decide how many improvements need to be made. Make your first offer a good offer, but never try to low ball the homeowners. Be realistic, and do not let your expectations get the best of you.

Understanding Mortgage Contracts - Mortgage contracts can be difficult to understand, but it's all about getting the terminology down and asking questions and/or doing research on things for which you would like a bit more understanding. The most important aspect of your mortgage to understand is the type of rate you'll be adhering to. Is it an Adjustable Rate Mortgage (ARM) or a Fixed Rate Mortgage (FRM)? An ARM means that the interest rate will change occasionally along with market conditions, while a FRM means that the interest rate stays the same.

While foreclosure is not something you want to deal with, you should at least read and review the terms. Typically, once you miss three payments, your lender can put the loan into default and foreclosure proceedings can start.

Attorney Review of Mortgage Papers - Terms and laws vary from state-to-state, but in New Jersey, your contract will contain an attorney review clause if a realtor prepared the paperwork. The clause states that you have three days – weekends and legal holidays do not count – to have the paperwork reviewed and given the okay by someone who is authorized to give you legal advice. Should the lawyer not approve of the contract, the realtor must be contacted within the three day time frame and the contract is deemed broken. If it's after the three day limit or there was no notice given of the disapproval, the contract remains legally binding. Regardless of the particular attorney review terms in your state, it's always a good idea to have your attorney thoroughly review the contracts anyway.

How GKRE can help you buy a home or property in NJ

With more than a decade of experience, Glen Kelly and his team of highly experienced agents is who you want by your side for the home buying process. While some settle for dispensing ordinary services, GKRE go above and beyond for their clients. Backed by powerful designations like SFR®, SRES®, and myself being a CRS® agent, we stand tall above our colleagues as true professionals in our field. You can't beat the level of quality, care, efficiency, and results that GKRE provides. GKRE will not rest until you have the keys to your dream home in your hand, and they'll help you through the entire process with all the care, consideration, and effort that they would give to their own family.

Chapter 5

Home Inspections

You've submitted the offer on a house you love, and it was accepted by the homeowner. If you thought the home-buying process was done, you are not there quite yet. Next up is the home inspection where an inspector will go through the home and check for issues that the current homeowners may not even know exist. Take everything step-by-step and you'll get through the home inspection process smoothly and in as little time as possible. Considering how big of a purchase buying a home is, it's certainly not something you want to take lightly or rush.

Choosing a Home Inspector

The home inspection is major, and the last thing you want to do is choose an inspector who could not give an adequate evaluation of a dog house. There are thousands of inspectors across the United States, and only about half of the states require certification, so how do you know which one is the best to choose? Here's how to decide.

Find an inspector early - Your contract will likely state how long you have to get the home inspection completed, but you do not want to rush and just settle for the first one who can get it done within that time frame. To make it easier on yourself and just get it off your mind, start looking for an inspector when you start looking for a home. That way, you can take your time doing the research without feeling overwhelmed.

Look for someone licensed - As stated above, only half of the states require home inspectors to be licensed, but even if they do have a license, it does not necessarily mean they are any good. The amount of training varies from state-to-state. However, an inspector holding a license is at least a step in the right direction. In respect to NJ, licensure is required. Select a New Jersey licensed home inspector.

Do searches through an organization - Each state has an organization where you can search for a home inspector on their website. For example, if you visit the website for the New Jersey Association of Licensed Professional Home Inspectors, you'll see the "Find an Inspector" link on the front page where you can search by name or county. You'll be able to view each inspector's contact info, and in some cases, their bio if they chose to write one.

Do Internet searches - As part of your research, do not hesitate to do an Internet search of the inspector's name. You'll likely see several professional pages, but you never know what else you could turn up in the process.

Ask your realtor - Your agent can give you some excellent recommendations. You should ask for around three recommendations to ensure you'll likely have at least one or two you'll feel comfortable working with you. Make sure to do your own research on them to see what is said. Remember your Realtor works with several home inspectors daily.

Ask the tough questions – Do not just have the inspector check out the home and let him leave. You have to ask several questions and any inspector who is professional and reputable will have no problem staying to answer you. For example, ask how many inspections they've done since they started, how many they've done in the past year, how long they've been in business, and if they have any complaints against them. You should also ask what their home inspection covers and if they offer repairs based on the results of the inspection.

Call for complaints - Each state has their own place to call to find out if the inspector you are thinking of hiring is legit and has anything in his background you should know about. For example, in New Jersey, you would contact the Home Inspection Advisory Committee. Even if the inspector says he has no complaints against him, it's best to call anyway and find out for yourself.

Once you have the attorney review completed, get moving on the home inspection. It may seem like a hassle to jump from one obligation to another, but consider it just one more step closer to you moving into your new home. Make sure to read the contract to find out exactly how long you have to get everything completed so you do not find yourself caught in a sticky situation.

Types of Home Inspection

Did you know there's more than one type of home inspection? There are those who think a general home inspection will include everything wrong with the home in minute detail, but that's not completely the case. The inspector will check out everything from windows and doors to patios and driveways, but if he spots anything specific that could prove extra detrimental, he'll recommend that you contact a specialist inspector. Before scheduling the inspection, consult with the homeowner about what time and dates work for them. You should always be present for whatever inspection is taking place, not only to make sure the job is being done correctly, but also just to gather information for your own knowledge. Depending on the size of your home, the inspection will take 1 – 3 hours, and typically, you'll have to pay for services once they are rendered. Even if the homeowners hand over their own inspection report, such as one from a pest control agency, get one yourself anyway. Unfortunately, you never know if they are trying to hide certain issues that could devalue their home. While the general inspection is one particular type, there are several others you may want to consider.

Pest inspection - Should you desire, you can contact a pest control company and ask them to do an inspection for various little critters that could cause you problems down the road, especially termites. Considering many people at some point have dealt with a pest control issue, do not hesitate to ask your family and friends for personal recommendations. Most home inspectors offer a combination of home and termite inspections, which is a smart idea to get.

Radon testing - Radon is a colorless, odorless, tasteless, and radioactive gas and it comes in through openings that have direct contact with the ground, such as through cracks in the foundation. The only way you'll know if it's in your home is through a specialized radon test. Surprisingly, radon is the second leading cause of lung cancer in the United States with thousands dying from it every year. It is to your benefit that you get it done.

Chimney inspection - If you are planning on using the fireplace, you should get the chimney inspected. You do not want to wait until you light up the fireplace to find out that there are problems you never knew existed. The inspector will make sure the inside of the chimney is in good condition and that the smoke can easily get out.

Mold inspection - You do not want to buy a home only to later find out that there's been mold growing in the walls. If the water damage was relatively recent, the homeowners may not even know yet that mold is growing, which is where a mold inspection comes in handy. An inspector will do an air quality test as well as do a test for mold and moisture.

After the Home Inspection: Repair Requests

The home inspection is essentially a list of repair requests for the homeowners to do before the transaction is officially completed. Some requests can be as simple as fixing a tile in a bathroom to something major like fixing the electrical wiring. You are likely not going to get all of the repairs fixed, but depending on your list, there's a good chance you could get most of them done. So how do you go about making the requests while increasing your chances of getting as many of the repairs done as possible without the cost of them having to come from your pocket?

Decide what's important to you - Some repairs you may deem absolutely necessary to fix, like plumbing issues, while others, like changing the carpeting in the living room, are basically part of your wish list. Once you get the inspection report back, think about what your needs are on the list and what you can go without fixing and you'll just do it yourself at a later date.

Let the inspector do the talking – It is one thing for the homeowners to hear about the list of repairs from you, but it's another when they are hearing it from the person who actually came up with the list in the first place. He'll be able to thoroughly explain to the homeowner about the issues whereas you may not fully be able to without coming off as biased.

Decide on a resolution - The decision is between you, the homeowner, and the lender. For example, the seller may agree to give the buyer a check for a chunk of the repairs once the house closes, but the buyer has to pay for the rest of the cost. Once you have the inspection report in front of you, all the parties involved can work it out. Before you get angry if the homeowners do not abide by all your requests, think of a way that you can work together. Try to see things from the seller's point of view, and what you can do on your end to make the situation easier and to move it along more quickly. In case of a problem, seek advice from your real estate agent who will certainly be able to point you in the right direction in terms of negotiation.

How GKRE Can Help With the Home Inspection Process

The home inspection process may seem simple enough, but it actually consists of a lot of small parts, all of which Glen Kelly and his team at GKRE are extensively trained to help you solve. From recommending inspectors to helping you understand the terminology in the reports, they'll be at your side throughout it all. Should you have any questions, those at GKRE will be happy to answer them and make the process as easy for you as possible.

Chapter 6

NJ Appraisals, Property Surveys and Flood Elevation Certifications

The papers are in, inspection is done, and you are almost at the finish line that ends right in front of your own home. There are a few more steps, the finishing touches if you will, to finally start to close the books on the home-buying process. Next up are appraisals, surveys, and certifications. All may seem boring and unnecessary in the grand scheme of things, but they protect you and reassure the lender that they will not get stuck in a mess.

What is an Appraisal?

An appraisal is a must in the mortgage process, and it's essentially the dollar amount that banks and mortgage companies put on a property for which a homeowner wants a loan. The lender will get the report to ensure that the loan they are providing is worth it when compared to the value of the property. If something happens where the borrower fails to pay the loan, the lenders have a viable property – your home – as a backup.

Consider the appraiser an objective third party who is licensed by the state and has no personal ties to the homeowner or buyer. They walk around the home and write down what they deem to be the value of the home. Each appraisal costs about $400 and is paid for by the person applying for the loan.

There are two parts to the appraisal – the "comps" and the breakdown of each aspect of the property, both of which comprise the Uniform Residential Appraisal Report (URAR). Comps, also known as comparables, compare your property to recently sold properties in your neighborhood, and are put together to complete a Comparative Market Analysis (CMA). The breakdown looks at everything on the property, from the landscaping on the outside to the appliances on the inside. While the comps take the real estate market approach, the breakdown takes the personal home approach. What it comes down to be the better your property is, from the inside out, the more of a chance you have of getting a high appraisal, and in turn, getting the loan you need and want.

How to Get a High Appraisal

The key to getting a high appraisal is to make the home and property look as updated, loved, and cared for as possible. It may not seem like little things matter, but it's all relevant when they come together to help you get a good appraisal. So what can you do to ensure the home is given the highest value possible?

Change your light fixtures - Light fixtures are some of the most prominent features of a home, and they can change the entire look and feel of a room. Update the fixtures as well as the light bulbs; make them energy efficient as they can take up less electricity and cost you less in the long run. Bathrooms and kitchens are at the top of the list for appraisers, so pay special attention to the lights used in the bathroom above the mirror. Make them as flattering as possible.

Do not have expectations based on neighbor's homes - There are some who think of comps as their next door neighbor's home, but not all houses are created equal. The key is to compare your home to other houses that are similar, not necessarily ones on either side of you. If you compare your home to your neighbor's pristine home that has a finished basement, three bedrooms, large granite counter-tops in the kitchen, energy efficient appliances, and more square footage; while you have an unkempt attic, two bedroom, little counter space in the kitchen, and outdated appliances, they are not going to result in the same value.

Change the appliances - If you have outdated appliances, not only are they likely unattractive, but they are also not energy efficient. Both factors could result in a lower appraisal. If possible, change the stove and refrigerator first. Should you be unable to get new appliances, update the ones you already have. Contact the respective manufacturers and ask if they sell face panels that you can change out with your existing ones. Another option is to use faux finishes, such as faux stainless steel film that you can put over your current appliances. It's a great way to match the appliances to each other. Be honest that they are not stainless steel, but the sleek look will definitely count for something.

Get rid of stains - Not only are they unsightly, but they are not going to do wonders for the overall appraisal. If you have stains on the carpeting, walls, or anywhere else where they are clearly visible, do your best to get rid of them rather than hide them.

Change your windows and doors - If any of your windows or doors do not open or close properly, or the frames are rotted, it's time to change them out. It's especially the case if there's a draft coming in through them. Not only do they make the rooms feel uncomfortable, but they can increase the heating or cooling bills exponentially. You should especially change them if the glass, frames, or doors have any cracks in them.

Fix any leaks or cracks in the exterior - Minor cracks in the foundation typically are not a big deal, and can easily be fixed, which a good idea is if you are planning on getting an appraisal. Horizontal cracks, ones that wrap around corners or wide cracks are another story. It's a good idea to have a specialized inspector look at them to see what your next course of action should be.

Change up the flooring - Hardwood floors are typically the most desirable flooring. If you have carpet covering it up; consider removing it so the wood is exposed. So many love it not only for its beauty, but it can complement almost any style of décor and is easier to keep clean and allergen-free than carpet.

Add new security features - Are all the carbon monoxide detectors and smoke detectors in working order? Are the locks properly working on the windows and doors? Do you have an excellent security system for the house? If the answer is "no" to any of the questions, then you may want to consider an upgrade. People want to feel safe and secure, especially in their own home, and it's going to do great things for the appraisal as well.

Clean up the front of the home - How the front of the house looks compared to how everything works on the inside may not seem like a big deal, but the property looks are the first thing people see when they look in the direction of your house. If the weeds are overgrown, the shutters are hanging off, a gutter is visibly loose, and the paint is peeling, your home is going to look more like something out of a horror movie than something that's going to be valued for a high amount. It does not take a lot of money to make it look its best. Start with the landscaping – trim the hedges and trees, mow the lawn, remove the weeds, and add some flowers or plants. Fix any loose pieces on the house – such as gutters, shutters, shingles, etc. – and change out the front door. If changing the front door is too expensive, paint it. Lastly, if you can paint the house a neutral color, that's even better.

Clear out the clutter - Again, the clutter does not count against you as much as a major internal issue, but it can make your home appear more beautiful, airy, and bigger, all of which certainly will not hurt when it comes to the appraisal. Do not just pack all the clutter away; it's just going to be a burden you'll have to deal with later on. Use this as an opportunity to get rid of what you do not need or want.

Overall, things like small carpet stains or an overgrown bush in the front will not count nearly as much against you as something major, like bad electrical wiring, but it will not help you either. When you fix the little things, they work out to something big, which is a fabulous overall look to your home and a higher appraisal.

During the Appraisal: What to Do and What You Need

When the appraiser comes, you do not just show your face and call it a day. Your work does not stop just because theirs starts. Sure your home can speak a bit for itself, but it does not hurt if you help the situation along a little. While the appraiser is making their rounds, there's several ways you can make your home sound even better without annoying the person and driving them crazy.

Talk up your neighborhood's best assets - Has there been anything that's been the real talk of the town lately? Maybe there's a new school being built or new restaurants opening, but whatever it is, let the appraiser know about it. It makes your area sound more exciting, and can make your property come across as more appealing as well.

Get yourself and the pets out of the way - There's a difference between talking up your town and home, and following the appraiser around like a puppy. No one wants to try to do their job with someone staring over their shoulder, blabbing constantly, and not giving them enough space to do what they have to do. Not only does it make you look annoying, but the appraiser may take it as a sign that you are trying to distract them from something wrong with the house.

While you are at it, keep your pets out of the way as well. You love Fido, but the appraiser may be allergic, might not be a fan of dogs, or could just want to walk around without an animal running in between his legs. If possible, keep your pets in a spare room or in the backyard or better yet, have a family member or friend watch them at their home temporarily.

Show similar properties in the area - Comps can be one of your biggest assets for getting a high appraisal on your home. However, you can't get the sale info for just any home in your neighborhood; it has to be one that's similar to yours and was sold within a certain time frame. The more recently it was sold, the better, but no later than six months before. It should be as close to the same size as your house as possible, and around the same age. Get as many comps as possible and a minimum of three at least. It may seem like a lot of work, but it's definitely worth it. That is where a good, professional Realtor comes into play for you.

Have lists of repairs you've made - An appraiser is not going to walk into your house and know all the repairs you've made unless you tell them. Keep an itemized list of everything you've done to make your home better, even if it's something you deem insignificant, like getting new light fixtures. Write down what the repairs were, how much they cost, and about what date they were done. Having it all available when the appraiser walks in the door can mean a big boost in your home's value.

Cut the small talk - The appraiser does not care that your kids have the lead in the school play or that you are currently in a fight with your sister. All talk should be kept to the topic of your home. The appraiser is on a schedule and frankly does not have time to deal with small talk while they are trying to get everything done. It can also distract him from noticing all the great things about your home, which is not going to bode well in the appraisal.

Ask questions at the end - Write down a list as you go along if you have to. Do not hound the appraiser with questions while he's trying to do his job. He'll likely be quite happy to answer any questions you have, just when everything is all done and over with and he has the time and attention to devote to them.

Be nice - A kind attitude and treating the appraiser with respect can go a long way. It may even help your case. Overall, just treat him with respect.

What to do if you get a low appraisal

You've had the appraisal completed, and it's much lower than you thought. There are several reasons why it could have happened including they were an inexperienced appraiser, you overpriced your home, or you are a victim of a bad real estate market in your neighborhood. You are seconds away from panicking, crying, or a little bit of both, but before that happens, take a deep breath and know that there are several things you can do to make things better.

Talk to your realtor - A good real estate agent, like those at GKRE, will help you through the difficult situation and help you find a solution, even if it means going over the appraisal report. As soon as you find out you received a low appraisal, call your agent to discuss the next steps.

Go over the appraisal - The appraiser is human, and therefore, capable of making a mistake. Maybe the square footage of the home was under-reported or there was a bathroom inadvertently left out, but read through the entire report to see if you come across any discrepancies.

File an appeal - If you strongly feel that your home is worth much more than it was deemed in the appraiser's report, then filing an appeal may be a good course of action. Check with the report you got as you may already have the page you need to file the report. If not, call the appraiser's office and ask for one so you can get the process started.

Lower the price - The home could be overpriced, but lowering it could make a big difference. You may not be thrilled about it, but the buyer and lender get what they want, and in the end, you do too if you get the sale you desire.

Get a second appraisal - A second opinion can be especially helpful if the first appraiser was inexperienced and did not seem to know what they were doing. The second report could end up coming in higher than the first. Ask for a more experienced appraiser who can get the job done right.

A low appraisal is not the end of the world; it just means it's going to take a few more steps to get the job done. Keep the end goal in mind, for you to sell your home at a good price. Do everything in your power to change the situation for the better. Your real estate agent will help you along the way, but this may be one of the times you have to take a little bit of bad with the good. However, it does not mean you should roll over and settle. Do what you can first before you wave the white flag.

What is a Property Survey?

A property survey is exactly what it sounds like – a survey of your property. A surveyor comes in and maps out where everything is on your property including sheds, driveways, fences, garages, walls, and of course, your house. Before making any improvements to a house or property, especially if you just bought it, getting a survey done of the property can save you a lot of headaches in the long run.

Reasons to Get a Property Survey Done

There are those who are worried that a property survey may turn up findings that are not beneficial for them, but in actuality, it allows you to know exactly how much land you have, which could prevent you from dealing with a lot of issues in the future. It's better to know the truth than to have to wonder or assume and get caught off guard at a later date. There have been many disputes over property that could have easily been settled if there was a property survey done in the first place. The cost of a property survey varies depending on your location as well as the size of your property. Here are a few more reasons that may convince you to get a property survey.

You might have more land to work with - You never know if part of your neighbor's property is actually your own. For all you know, that tiny yard you currently have may actually stretch into the sprawling lot next to you. Not only is it great in terms of space, but also in terms of value of your home.

You save yourself from arguments - There have been many neighbors who have had fights over whose land is whose and what belongs where. For example, one neighbor may have placed a fence on what he thought was his property when his neighbor is saying that it's on his land. Get a land survey done and the argument is over and done with within minutes rather than stretched out over time.

You might have less land than you thought - While it could turn out you have more land than you thought, it might be the other way around as well. The survey could prove that your neighbor actually owns some of your land that you've thought was yours all this time. At least you'll know exactly what you are working with once the survey is completed.

Discrepancies could affect the value of your property - If you have the exact amount of land you thought, then a survey is going to keep your property value the same, but if you have more or less, it's going to have an effect. It'll be good for you to know either way so you can have accurate information on your home and property.

You are legally protected - A neighbor could sue you stating that your garage you built or tree you planted is on their property, but if you get the survey done and it turns out they are wrong, it could work out in your favor. The surveyor may even be called to testify on your behalf if your neighbor is still giving you a problem.

What is a Flood Elevation Certificate?

If you've never heard of a flood elevation certificate, you are not alone. Unless you live in a designated flood area, you may never hear of it unless you've built a new home. It's essentially what is used to determine the premium paid for flood insurance. In order to rate homes built after the Flood Insurance Rate Map (FIRM), the flood elevation certificate is required. However, if your home was built before publication of FIRM and you are located in a flood area; your home can still be rated.

Only an architect, land surveyor, or engineer who is authorized by the state or local government to certify flood elevation information can issue a flood elevation certificate.

How GKRE Can Help You

All the work with appraisals, surveys, and certificates could make you feel overwhelmed and as if it's all too much to deal with, but just remember that GKRE is there to help you with any questions or concerns you have. GKRE has years of experience in the industry, and has dealt with their fair share of all of the aforementioned, not only with clients, but also for themselves as well. GKRE will not steer you wrong, and you can count on them to get you through the slew of final steps in the home-buying process to make it as easy and painless for you as possible so you can finally get into your new home.

Chapter 7

Mortgage Commitments

A mortgage commitment is the official letter from your lender or bank stating that you (finally!) got the funds you were hoping for after all this time. It's a seemingly simple piece of paper that can change everything, and it's the sign that the long process is almost over. However, you want the process to go as smoothly as possible, and it all starts with who you choose for a mortgage broker.

Reasons to Hire a Licensed Mortgage Broker

The mortgage broker is the middle man between you and your lender. They must be trusted to pass along information in a timely and efficient manner, and are going to prove useful to you in the long run. If that's not enough, there are several more reasons why hiring a mortgage broker is the best idea.

They know a slew of lenders - It's a mortgage broker's job to know lenders, so chances are they know a lot more than you will just by doing research. Once they see your paperwork, they will already have a name or two in mind of someone with whom would work perfectly for you.

Less hassle finding your perfect lending match - As stated above, the mortgage broker knows a lot of lenders, and will be able to help you find the perfect one for you. You would then have to follow that up with comparing all the information they gave you, processing it, and making the best decision. Your other option would be for you to look them up yourself or get personal recommendations, but you would need to do your research and then make all the phone calls.

More time saved on your part - Take a quick glance over the last paragraph. Now just imagine how much time it's going to take you to do the research, make all the calls, do the comparisons, and ultimately make the best decision. Think about how much you already have to do in a day. The mortgage broker can save you a ton of extra time, and considering their expertise in the field, they can get it done much more quickly than you could.

They deal with hassles so you do not have to - Calling different lenders and doing research does not just take up a lot of time, it's also going to cause you a lot of hassle and headaches. A mortgage broker deals with these things for a living and knows how to navigate their way through the hassles with ease. Considering you have less experience dealing with this particular situation, it's going to be a bit more of a rocky path and will probably last you much longer than you expect to get the final results.

You have an asset on your side - Not only does the mortgage broker have a ton of experience, but they also will not get paid until the loan is completed, which means they are extremely motivated to get you the results you are happy with in a timely manner. It's also going to be useful to have an additional resource that you can go to if you have any questions about the process.

What Makes a Good Mortgage Broker?

It's not enough to just find a mortgage broker, you have to choose one who is actually worth dealing with and is going to help you get the results you want and need. So what exactly makes a good mortgage broker stand out from all the rest?

They are licensed - If a mortgage broker is not licensed, move on. To find out if the mortgage broker is licensed, contact the respective agency in your state. For example, in New Jersey, you would contact the New Jersey Department of Banking & Insurance (Licensing Services Bureau) for more information.

They come highly recommended - Chances are your family and friends have used a mortgage broker at some point. Before you start doing your own research, reach out and see what you can find out from them. Take notes, and if you get several recommendations for a specific one, contact that person first.

They answer all your questions without a problem - A good mortgage broker will not give you grief or roll their eyes at you if you ask a question (or ten). They'll answer them happily, knowing that it's not only your mortgage on the line, but also their paycheck.

They go over all the fine print with you - A mortgage broker who is great at their job is not going to hand over a bunch of papers to you and expect that you are going to read through it all and understand everything that's going on. They are going to go over it with you, read through the fine print, explain all the fees and costs, and answer any questions you have. They'll be straightforward with you rather than try to rush you out of their office.

They effectively communicate with you - In addition to answering your questions and being honest with you, a good mortgage broker can easily be reached whether it's by phone or email. When you call and leave a message, they respond back to you in a timely manner. It's not days before you hear from them, but usually hours. They do not talk down to you or speak in condescending manner even when you do not understand something, but instead, talk with you about what is going on.

They act in your best interest - Despite how the mortgage broker does not get paid if the loan does not go through, you should not feel as though they are only in it for the paycheck. You need to feel as though you can count on them. That they always have your best interests in mind and they will make moves on your part that are always followed through.

They under-promise and over-deliver - If a mortgage broker is promising you things left and right, you may want to really evaluate if dealing with them is worth it. Too many promises may make them appear as though they can't be trusted. The only promise they should make is that they'll do the best they can for you and will help you get the best results. Essentially, they should under-promise and over-deliver.

They have a lot of education and experience - When you are dealing with something as important as a mortgage, you want a mortgage broker who has education and experience. Someone who does not just settle for what they have, but also builds on it. They should have a fully complete background while also continuing taking classes and seminars, strengthening their client base, and building up their reputation.

How GKRE Can Help You

Those at GKRE have years of experience, and they are not just going to stand by and let you fend for yourself with finding a mortgage broker. It's a big decision, and one that they can certainly help you with. Each real estate agent can recommend several mortgage brokers that are right for you and your situation, help you with any questions you have, and get you even further on your way to being in your brand new home.

Chapter 8

Homeowners Insurance and Flood Insurance

Insurance is an essential part of owning a home, and two of the primary types you'll need to look into are Homeowners Insurance and Flood Insurance. They are not as exciting as getting handed the keys to your house or shopping for the furniture, but they can cover all those nice things you carefully chose to put in your new home, as well as, the structure itself in case disaster strikes. So what exactly do you need to know about Homeowners Insurance and Flood Insurance?

What is Homeowners Insurance?

Homeowners Insurance is what protects your home and everything you have in it should disaster strike, such as fires, hurricanes, and certain types of storm damage. The policy covers the loss of your personal belongings, such as clothes and furniture, and damage to the inside and outside of your home, including structures such as garages and sheds. If there's any injury or damage caused by you or a member of your family, such as if your son accidentally breaks your neighbor's window with a baseball, it might be covered under your policy. You'll also be covered for personal liability if you are sued. In the case of a disaster where you can't live in your home and you are forced to stay in a rental house or a hotel, you'll be covered for all the costs incurred during the time you were displaced. This includes not only the cost of staying in a temporary dwelling, but also for your meals and some other certain expenses. However, there are cost limits, so it's important to carefully review your policy before you book the nicest suite in town.

What you need for Homeowners Insurance

The average cost of Homeowners Insurance varies from state-to-state. For example, in New Jersey as of September 2013, the average cost was $862, while in New York its $722 and in Pennsylvania its $727. Florida has one of the highest averages in the country with $1,192.

The extent of the information you'll have to provide your agent also varies from state-to-state, but you'll typically need to provide the square footage of the house, a description of the interior and exterior, the number of rooms and stories, the age, and the type of security protection you have.

Before you purchase any Homeowners Insurance, you'll be able to talk to an agent, review all the different policies, and get a free quote of how much you could pay depending on the policy you choose.

What Is Flood Insurance?

Flood insurance is what you can purchase to protect your home from a variety of flood-related damage. It's important to note that regular water damage and flood damage coverage are two completely separate things. If you live in a designated flood area, you will be required to purchase flood insurance, but if you do not, you can still buy it if you want that extra peace of mind. Even if you rent and do not own, you can still buy it.

Like Homeowners Insurance, Flood Insurance covers damage to your home as well as your possessions. However, should you get flooded out of your home and are forced to temporarily take up residence elsewhere; those expenses are not covered under the plan. Some think that flood insurance will cover all the loss and damage, but it does not; there's a cap for what's actually covered. The Federal Flood Insurance cap for residential homes is $250,000, so if the structure of your home is damaged and it's worth more than that amount, you are out of luck for anything above that cap. For personal possessions, the cap is $100,000. Your Homeowners Insurance policy may not even cover flood-related damage, so if your home is worth more than $250,000, you should look into additional coverage just in case, especially if you live in a designated flood area. You should also be aware that hot tubs and swimming pools – above ground and below – are not covered under Flood Insurance.

With flood insurance and home owner's insurance policies, it is vital to read over the entire policy cover-to-cover to find out what exactly is covered under your particular plan, especially before you sign on the dotted line and hand over a check to enroll.

How GKRE Can Help You

Real estate agents at GKRE are not just about selling you a home and going on their way. They are there to make sure you have everything else you need to live comfortably, safely, and with a great peace of mind. Being that GKRE is located in Ocean County right near the Jersey Shore; they are well-versed in everything having to do with Flood Insurance.

With two flood zones in New Jersey – A-zone and V-zone – there's now a less designated flood zone areas thanks to the new FEMA revised flood maps of 2013, and it could be a bit confusing if you are not familiar with all the changes. For example, in Ocean County where GKRE is located, there were once 38,012 acres of V-zones; now it's been reduced to 20,808. All of the agents are up-to-date on the latest information, and can help you with any questions or concerns you may have, whether or not you are in a designated flood area. You will not have to worry about navigating the insurance process on your own when you have GKRE on your side.

Chapter 9

Certificate of Occupancy Inspection

If you've never heard of a Certificate of Occupancy (CO) or a Certificate of Continued Occupancy (COO), you should familiarize yourself with the terms if you are getting ready to buy property. Some think they are only issued to commercial buildings, but the certificates are actually for residential dwellings as well. Other than knowing they are two very important pieces of paper, what are they and what should you know about them?

What is a Certificate of Occupancy (CO)?

The Certificate of Occupancy (CO) is a paper document stating that a new building is up to code in accordance with the law. It's issued by the local government, and deems that the property is ready to live in.

A visual inspection is necessary in order to obtain the CO, which means the inspector will not physically test out everything to make sure it's safe and in working order, but will be able to tell visually. There will be a walkthrough of your home, and the inspector will look at everything that could cause a safety concern. For example, they will check that there are smoke detectors on all floors and that they are in working order, that carbon monoxide detectors are present in sleeping areas, that there are railings on all sets of stairs, and that all the appliances are working properly.

Some townships simply require inspection of working smoke detectors, carbon monoxide detectors, and visual inspection of a charged fire extinguisher installed in the Kitchen, while some other townships require significantly more to be inspected prior to receiving the CO for closing.

The inspector will also keep an eye out for other safety concerns, such as a bug infestation, a mold problem, a cracked foundation, and rotting wood. The inspection is not just inside, but outside as well, which means there should be no safety hazards on the premises. For example, check that your pool has a safety cover, that there are no loose stones on your walkway, that all trim around windows and doors is completely intact, and that old wells are properly cared for by standards.

If there's something in or around your home that the most obsessive person would deem a safety concern, write it down and make sure it's taken care of. It's better to tackle everything at once rather than have to deal with a re-inspection. The inspection for the CO happens quickly, typically within four days of you making the call, so make sure all the issues are fixed before you even schedule the appointment. Typically, the fee for a CO is under $200 (depending on the township).

What is a Certificate of Continued Occupancy (CCO)?

When you rent or sell your existing home, you'll need a Certificate of Continued Occupancy (CCO). It costs typically below $150 to obtain, and is the responsibility of the current homeowner. You would apply for the CCO before applying for the CO, and it's typically good for about three months.

The inspection for the CCO is similar to that for the CO. Some things that the inspector will look out for are that all house numbers are clearly visible from the street, all windows and doors are working properly, the structure overall must be safe from floor-to-roof, there must be fire extinguishers present in or very close to the kitchen area, and there must be smoke detectors and carbon monoxide detectors present. As a note, septic systems are approved by the Health Department. As stated with the CO, walk around your home and use your most discerning eye possible. If you think the inspector could pick up on it with his trained eye, you are better off taking care of it before the inspection.

How GKRE Can Help You

As simple as a CO or a CCO inspection may be, it can be overwhelming when you start thinking if you missed anything, if something will go awry, or that you are not going to walk away with the important piece of paper. Let the agents at GKRE take some of the stress off you. They are skilled with handling inspections and pressure, they know what the inspectors are looking for and can help you get everything ready so you'll be able to pass with flying colors. Have any questions? They will not hesitate to help you with whatever you need.

Chapter 10

Mortgage Payoffs, Walk-through Inspection, and Closing

You can see the finish line in front of you, and you are so close to being able to move into your new home that you can barely stand it. Only a few more roadblocks and you are set. Are you ready to finally get the keys to your new home? If so, keep reading to find out how to deal with your next steps in the process that involves the mortgage payoff, the walk-through inspection, and the closing.

What is a Mortgage Payoff Statement?

The mortgage payoff statement is prepared by the lender and states the terms of your mortgage, including how much you owe and your interest rate. While you are obviously excited to get your new home, this little piece of paper can drain a bit of that from you once you get a look at what's on it. No one likes looking at dollar signs unless it involves income.

In order to get the mortgage payoff statement, you can either call your lender to speak with them directly, get it online or some lenders have made it even more convenient where you can call their automated system and request it even when no one is in the office. Make sure to hold onto all of the records for tax purposes.

What is a Final Inspection Walk-through?

Final inspection is such a nice term at this point isn't it? After all the searching, researching and paperwork, you feel like everything is really coming together. The final inspection walk-through is done within days of closing, and gives you another chance to make sure everything is just what you wanted and were promised. Some buyers do not like to do it the day of the actual closing so that if any issues should arise, you are faced with having to hold off on the process; so they do it at least a day or two ahead of time. You do not actually have to do the final inspection, but you absolutely should, especially with something as big of an investment as a house.

While you are doing the walk-through, bring a list of repairs that were supposed to be made, and check to make sure they were actually done. If the seller of the home agreed to make them, they should have been done by that time. Also, take a look around for any other issues that just do not seem right considering the home is going to be in its bare form. You've likely only seen it stuffed with furniture, but when you see it without the entire owner's personal items; you can really get a good view at what everything looks like from floor-to-ceiling. Keep in mind, however, that you can't renegotiate the contract and suddenly decide you want them to add a new ceiling fan just because you think the place looks a little too empty.

While you are doing the walk-through, do not just check on things that needed repairs, take a look at everything you are going to be using on a daily basis just to make sure that nothing happened to them since the previous inspection. For example, check all the windows and doors, try out the appliances that are being left behind, testing out the heating and cooling, and turning on all the lights. Do not forget to turn the water on and off and check that the toilets flush. Also, make sure that there was no damaged done in the process of them moving their items out of the house, such as new scratches on the hardwood floors or cracked paint from a heavy couch knocking into it.

What Happens at a Closing?

This is the moment you've been waiting for! Well, besides actually moving your furniture in and finally feeling like the home is yours. The closing is when all the papers are signed, and the house officially goes from being someone else's property to becoming your own home. Make sure a couple days before the scheduled closing, call all the utility companies and turn on / switch service into your name for said closing date.

When you go to officially sign the papers, bring a binder filled with all the paperwork you've accumulated during the process just in case a last-minute issue arises. It likely will not, but just in case, you'll be prepared anyway. It's at this point you'll also hand over a check to cover all the closing costs. You are also going to receive several more documents to add to your binder, including a HUD Statement, the lease or deed, the mortgage paperwork, the TILA statement, and the CO or CCO.

There are usually quite a few people at the closing other than yourself and the seller. Both of you will each have an attorney present, a closing agent, a notary public, both your real estate agents, and your lender's representative may also be there.

Before you even put pen to paper, make sure you read through absolutely everything and really know what you are signing. Do not get so excited that you put your signature on the dotted line and find out later there's something you should have questioned.

Congratulations, because once you sign your name, the home is now officially yours.

What is a HUD Statement?

The HUD Statement, also known as the HUD-1 Settlement Statement, is a summary of all the funds that have exchanged hands pertaining to the closing, and it's completed by the closing agent. It's an itemized list of the seller and buyer's transactions, as well as, all the final charges and fees associated with the closing process. Both the seller and the buyer get a copy. The form is used at every real estate closing as part of the Real Estate Settlement Procedures Act (RESPA).

If you take a look at the HUD-1 Settlement Statement form, you'll notice that sections B through H pertain to the basic information about the buyer, seller, and lender. Other important sections are section J which discusses the buyers' costs, section K discusses the financial transactions of the seller and section L on page 2 details all the settlement charges, including broker fees and title charges. Also, review page 3 which breaks down the Good Faith Estimate charges (GFE) and the HUD-1 charges, as well as, the loan terms. Do not assume everything on the paper is correct. Closing agents are human, which means they can make mistakes. Go over it with your attorney to ensure all information is correct before you okay it.

How GKRE Can Help

All of the final steps of the house buying process can seem more than intimidating, but those at GKRE will be at your side to help you. Whether it's going with you for the final walk-through or helping you review the HUD-1 Statement, they'll answer any questions you have, ensure you are getting just what you were promised, and that all your interests are being protected. You can have peace of mind knowing that you have reputable and experienced agents to help you through the process.

Chapter 11

New Construction

Maybe a pre-existing home is not for you. You might want a place that's never been lived in before, one that has all the trademarks of your particular style, and one where you are not going to have to worry that there's hidden problems behind the walls you have not yet discovered. It also feels pretty special to know you are the starting point for making memories in the house. Having a new home built is a huge investment, but one that can really pay off in the long run. Keep reading to find out how to get the process started. Glen Kelly Real Estate is an expert in NJ new home construction.

How to Find a Good Builder

The first step in having a home built is finding a good builder. After all, finding one that has shoddy skills and an even worse reputation is just as bad as buying a pre-existing house that has mold growing in the walls and hardwood floors darkened with various stains and scratches. Even if you've never had to look for a builder before, there are several ways to get started that can help you begin to develop the home of your dreams.

Ask for personal recommendations - Use social networking to your advantage. Make a post and ask for personal recommendations from family and friends. Even if they've never had a home of their own built, they may know someone who has, and you'll be able to get good insight into how the builder was.

Ask the builder for references – Do not hesitate to ask for at least 4 or 5 references for homes the builder has done in the past, and make sure you follow up and check them out. If he does not give them to you, let it go and move onto someone else. When you call to check on the references, ask to set up a meeting so you can view the home for a few moments and ask a few questions about the job. Should you be unable to meet in person, have a list of questions ready to ask over the phone.

Check the credentials - Visit the website of the National Association of Homebuilders and take a look at their directories. You'll be able to do a search of exactly what you want and view each builder's designation as well as their designation year and contact information.

Go with experience - A less-experienced builder may be cheaper, but it's often that you get what you pay for. Always go with experience, someone who knows what they are doing. You are going to have to live in that home, and it's a big responsibility to trust someone to build it for you. It should be someone who has done numerous top-quality homes built with clients satisfaction.

Choose the type of builder you want - The type of builder you'll call depends on the type of home you want. For example, if you want a completely new home built from scratch where you get exactly what you want and they know how to get and provide it to you, then go with a custom builder. If you like the idea of going with a pre-designed home and incorporating your own ideas, a semi-custom builder is for you. They'll start with their own design, but are willing to work with you to put in the type of look and details you desire. Lastly, you can go with a production home buyer, who essentially builds the type of home a building firm wants, and if you want any changes, it's going to cost you quite a bit of money and time to get it done to your specifications.

Ask your real estate agent - Your agent should be an expert when it comes to finding professionals to help you design the type of home that you want, and those at GKRE can certainly provide results. Do not hesitate to ask your real estate agent for personal recommendations of builders, however, just make sure you follow up and do your research anyway if only for your peace of mind.

Look at the Better Business Bureau - The BBB makes it really easy to search for a builder's name and pull up their rating as well as if they've ever had any complaints against them in the past. An A+ rating is the best while F is the worst. If you see an NR, it means that no rating was given for one reason or another, such as there was not a sufficient amount of paperwork provided.

Look up customer ratings - There are plenty of sites online that offer up customer ratings you are sure to find useful. There are obviously some fake reviews out there, so it's important to read through all of the reviews available and trust your gut as well as pair it up with the rest of the information you've found on a particular builder.

Doing your research may seem like a waste, a long and tedious process you do not need, but when you walk into your brand new home and you can feel safe and secure knowing that it was properly built and you have nothing to worry about. It will all be worth it.

Signs of a Good Builder

You've done all your research, and you are ready to finally choose a builder. Now it's time to consider who they are as a person and a professional. Are they going to get the work done efficiently and properly as well as treat you like a valued client that you are? There are several signs to watch out for that indicates your builder could be just what you've been looking for.

The builder is flexible - The whole reason you are having a custom home built is so you can get the type of home done that you want, so if the builder is not working with you, being flexible, and incorporating the types of changes and details that you want, then what's the point of working with him? A good builder will not hesitate to hear you out on your ideas, give you feedback, and ultimately try to do their best when giving you results.

They properly answer all your questions - If your builder is rolling their eyes when you ask "yet another question," then move on. Any builder worth their money is going to know that questions are all part of the process, and an important part at that. They'll take their time to answer any questions you have and explain the answers in terms you'll understand without making you feel foolish.

They back up their work - Problems happen during construction, but should it be your responsibility and come out of your pocket if they do? Absolutely not, a good builder will back up their work and fix any issues that arise without making it seem like the problem is yours to carry. Do not forget to make sure the warranty information is in writing in the contract before you sign on the dotted line.

They are easy to communicate with - Have you ever tried to talk to a supposed professional who will not return your calls in a timely manner, talked down to you, made you feel like you were just a dollar sign and overall, you just felt uncomfortable whenever you had to talk to them? If a builder is not easy to communicate with, it's only going to create problems for you in the long run that you definitely do not need.

He works on a good timetable - The builder should outline when he's going to start, when he's going to finish, and approximate dates for when each stage of the home-building process is going to be completed. Things may not go exactly according to plan as issues occasionally come up, but a good builder will always make every attempt to stick to the timetable without sacrificing quality of the finished product.

He belongs to a builders association - Belonging to a homebuilders association means that the builder has to adhere to their strict code of ethics in order to be a member. When researching builders, check to see what association they belong to. For example, in New Jersey, you would contact the New Jersey Builders Association (NJBA) for more information. Just note that just because a builder is not part of any particular association does not necessarily mean that they are not the right builder for you.   Rely more on references and your Realtors recommendation.

He outlines all the details without a problem - Any builder who is worth it is going to outline all their plans, not just the timetable, and make sure you are okay with everything that's planned. They are going to ask for your okay before proceeding, and should a problem arise during construction, a good builder will not hesitate to talk to you and come up with a new set of details and timetable to work with.

He does not sacrifice quality - A good builder you want to work with will not sacrifice quality for cost. Although builders could use materials that could save them and you thousands, it's worth it to have the best materials used that are going to result in a home that's safe, sturdy, and beautiful, and one you'll feel great living in without concerns for many years to come.

How to Find the Perfect Lot to Build On

Your land has just as much to do with your new home as the design of the house itself. After all, if your new home sits on bad land, the structure of the house could be compromised, and it may not even take long for it to happen. There's a lot you need to do and consider when you are looking for the perfect lot to build on.

Consider the size of the house - Is the size of the land adequate compared to the size of the house you want to buy? You should also factor in if you want to make any changes in the future, such as adding on an addition or putting a garage on the side or a shed in the back. If you think you want to make future changes, make sure you have the space should you decide to do so.

Think about location - Ask yourself if the location is ideal for you, especially in relation to where you and your spouse work, and if applicable, where your kids go to school. Sometimes even the nicest piece of land is not worth building on if it's going to be an inconvenience to you and your family.

Think about the price - Is the land something you can afford, especially when factored in with the cost of building the house, not to mention the upkeep? Make a list of all the money you'll have to shell out before you agree to purchase the land.

Ask for a soil test – Do not automatically assume that the soil is safe just because it does not seem like there's anything wrong with it. You want to make sure it's not contaminated, especially if you plan on creating a garden and eating the fruits and vegetables from it.

Consider the terrain - Is the land flat enough for you to build on? Is it going to be a safety concern for you if you build on it? All of these things are what you need to consider before you draw up plans for a new home.

Factor in zoning - You have to talk to someone from your local zoning board about the specifics for the land you want to buy. Your real estate agent can help with this as well. You'll have to find out just how far you can build from your property line as it varies depending on where you live.

Think about utilities - Does the land already have everything you need, including electricity, gas, water, and sewer, or are you going to have to set that up yourself? If so, expect to add quite a hefty total onto your budget if you have to make all the changes.

Consider the surrounding area - Do some digging and find out what the plans are for the area surrounding the land you want to buy. If there's a plan in the works to build a huge shopping mall, an airport, or a bunch of high rises that are going to block your spectacular view, your piece of land may not seem so great to you anymore.

When you are looking at a plot of land, it's best to have an architect and an engineer take a look at it before you put all your time, money, and energy into developing your dream home. You could save yourself quite a bit of hassle and heartbreak in the long run.

Phases of New Construction

There's a lot that goes into the construction of new homes. Look around your home and think about it. All the floors, walls, trim, counters, windows, etc., were once just the dream of a designer and had to be put into place. Every builder has their own set of stages that they follow, all of which are followed to the letter to ensure everything is done properly.

Preparation and planning - In this stage, you'll go over all the plans with the builder for what you want where and what you want done. From budget to design, everything is discussed and the process can get underway once you give the okay.

Foundation - Next up is the foundation stage that involves an excavation, underground plumbing being put in, and everything for the bottom floor of your home to be put in place, including your garage.

Framing -In the third stage, framework is put into place, trusses or roof rafters are set, and the walls start to really come together and look like an actual house structure.

Roofing and exterior - In the roofing and exterior phase is when it all comes together to really look like a house. The roof is completed, the windows and doors are put in place, and the exterior roof shingles and siding are completed.

Utilities - Now comes all the electrical, heating and cooling, and plumbing work. This is where the duct-work is installed as well as all the electrical wiring, and of course, the piping for plumbing.

Inspections – At every step of the way, city inspectors are going to take a look at how everything is going, make sure the builder is doing the building up to code, and give the stamp of approval that everything is going as it should.

Drywall and insulation - In this stage, drywall and insulation are put in, and tape and texture are added.

Design implementations - Your house is finally starting to look like a home. Railings, cabinetry, tiles, and counters are added, all with your okay of course. Paint is also added in this stage.

Final details - The final details stage is when the appliances are put in, carpet is put down, driveways are added, and additional final touches are included.

More inspections - There are more inspections to be completed, not only by city inspectors, but by you as well. This is the phase when you'll do the final walk through and make sure everything is as it's supposed to be and up to the quality that you were promised.

Closing - The best stage of them all – closing! This is when you review and sign all the documents and the home officially becomes yours. Congratulations!

How GKRE Can Help

Those at GKRE are not just your standard real estate agents. Glen himself has hands-on experience as a carpenter with a concentration in new home building. He apprenticed under his father, John Kelly, who himself is a master carpenter and a certified New Jersey licensed New Home Builder and owner of K & K Building and Remodeling LLC. Over the years, between his hands-on experience and knowledge obtained in the real estate market, Glen has become an expert in new home construction, and can help you with any questions or problems you come across. Rest assured that Glen Kelly teaches all of his agents and has mandatory training sessions on new construction in order to ensure every agent at Glen Kelly Real Estate is astute and well versed and always there to help you every step of the way.

Chapter 12

Short Sales and Foreclosures

When you purchase a home, you never intend to have financial difficulties and find yourself facing the possible loss of your home. However, it does happen, and it's best to be aware of what your options are should the situation arise. Ignoring the problem and hoping it goes away is not a good idea, but there are two options that could help you should you find yourself in financial straits.

What is a Short Sale?

A short sale is when the proceeds of selling the house equal to less than the mortgage and fees standing on the property. It's at this point when the borrower and lender come together to a resolution and agree that selling the property as is and taking a loss is a far better option than its current state of debt. If you decide on a short sale, you can then use the proceeds from the sale to pay off most, if not all of your current mortgage. This is a good option if you've tried almost everything else. For example, you can't refinance your mortgage, you can't sell your home despite trying, the debts are building up, and you really just want to leave and start fresh.

Difference between Short Sale and Foreclosure

Despite some thinking that a short sale and foreclosure is the same thing, the short sale is actually referred to as the pre-foreclosure. Overall, short sales have a better impact on your credit report than a foreclosure, and the latter is when you are left with absolutely no other options as the lender has officially seized the property. The process of foreclosure starts 90 days after you've missed your first mortgage payment. When it comes to selling the property, a real estate agent will take care of a short sale while the foreclosure property becomes the responsibility of the lender to put up for auction. There's also typically a lot more hassle with a foreclosure, from the buying and selling standpoint, than short sale properties.

Remember with a short sale the current seller still has title to the home (owns the property) so you as a buyer you are working with the seller and the sellers bank in order to get the bank to issue a short sale approval (sellers bank to accept less then what's currently owed on the home). In the case of a foreclosure the bank has already seized the home, taking title to the property, and as a buyer you are buying directly from the bank.

How GKRE Can Help

Dealing with a short sale or foreclosure is overwhelming, stressful, and can require a lot of paperwork and questions you may not want to take on yourself. The good news is that you have GKRE on your side. Every agent at GKRE is taught directly from Short Sales and Foreclosure Resource (SFR®) specialist, Glen Kelly. This means that they can expertly help you negotiate with lenders, limit your risk, and overall, protect your interests. They'll be able to answer any questions you have and walk you through the process with as little hassle as possible. When you are dealing with a short sale or foreclosure, you'll receive a wealth of knowledge, expertise, and assistance from every agent at GKRE.

Chapter 13

Careers in Real Estate

So you think you might want to pursue a career in real estate? That is a great decision.

Although real estate is not easy by any stretch of the imagination, it is a great profession.

Steps to take for becoming a NJ licensed Realtor:

1. Schedule to take a New Jersey real estate salesperson course at an approved school.

2. After successfully completing said coursework you will be allowed to take the state exam.

3. Upon passing the exam, you will get finger printed.

4. Select a Broker for whom you wish to work for and submit your application.

Sounds easy enough right? Well in actuality it is pretty tough to pass the class and the state test. Both require a lot of attention to detail and time on your part.

After you pass your state exam it is now time to setup interviews with a couple Brokers. You will be amazed how each Broker you meet runs their office differently then another Broker's office. Try to find a Broker that will cater to your specific needs. For example, if you require a lot of hands on training then select a Broker that is going to supply that.

Agents with my company are never mandated to do floor time (the industry standard), which means they are always focused on customer needs with a personalized, hands-on approach. They spend time doing what they do best – listing and selling homes, and helping the client get the most out of the process. Every agent that is part of Glen Kelly Real Estate is specially trained to provide only the best service to any buyer and seller.

If you decide to interview at Glen Kelly Real Estate here's what you can expect so you can easily compare with what other Brokers offer:

1. Glen Kelly Real Estate is different than the norm. You have to imagine a world where licensed real estate agents actually become a part of real estate history. The art of real estate is a business and should be treated as such. Glen Kelly, Realtors is always seeking

motivated, licensed agents that have a thirst for knowledge and professionalism.

2. Unlike most Brokers, notice that we advertise what we offer agents in plain view. No need to setup a meeting to find out what we offer. No wasted time, no hidden fees, no offers of ridiculous commission splits, just simply just the facts.

3. Glen Kelly, Realtors offers an exclusive, comprehensive training program for each and every agent where the broker actually takes an interest in the agent's success.

4. Glen Kelly, Realtors does not believe in company caravans and never wants agents to waste their time and money on caravans.

5. Glen Kelly, Realtors offers agents referral leads with no fee to the agent. Quite simply no agent will pay a referral fee for company leads. The company pays for advertising on trusted real estate sites and every agent is on a rotation for leads.

6. Glen Kelly, Realtors does not believe in desk or monthly fees, no office fees, no commission override fees, no E&O insurance fees, etc.

7. At Glen Kelly, Realtors the Broker of Record is a Certified Short Sale Specialist, Certified Residential Specialist, and Seniors Real Estate Specialist. The Broker of Record is on call for all agents at no extra charge or fee. The Broker of Record will help all agents will any and all listings and sales.

8. At Glen Kelly, Realtors there is never a fee for signs. Not only does the company pay for yard signs at all listings, but we actually install and take them down for the agent.

9. Glen Kelly, Realtors does not charge for lock boxes and supplies them for all listings.

10. Glen Kelly, Realtors has a firm stance against miscellaneous commission fees. There are no office, desk, copy, internet, etc. fees ever.

11. Glen Kelly, Realtors pays thousands upon thousands of dollars for advertising, including television ads.

12. One of the biggest differences at Glen Kelly, Realtors is we provide customizable, comprehensive training beyond compare to each agent. Our state of the art office hosts each training session. There is never a fee to attend any training classes.

No matter where you decide to hang your license, make sure you do your homework before joining just any company.

The business model at Glen Kelly, Realtors puts the business back in business plan. From our brand new office to our state of the art conference / board room, every single aspect of real estate is practiced with precise detail. Call Glen Kelly Real Estate at 732-244-0567 today and ask for an opportunity to speak with the Broker of Record for an interview.

Chapter 14

Conclusion

Those at Glen Kelly Real Estate do not just think of the real estate industry as a way to make a living; they also love what they do and consider it a real honor to help their clients sell, find or build the home of their dreams. At the end of the day, they know they helped others start a new chapter of their life in a home that they'll be happy to wake up in every morning.

We at GKRE invite you to contact our office and our New Jersey licensed real estate agents with any questions you have whether you are buying or selling. We are proud to serve New Jersey and its residents, and look forward to doing so for many years to come.

Thank you for all of your time. I wish you well in your real estate endeavors!

www.ingramcontent.com/pod-product-compliance
Lightning Source LLC
Chambersburg PA
CBHW081834170526
45167CB00007B/2795